ROMANCE & REVOLUTION

VANESSA MATIC

TOUGH POETS PRESS
ARLINGTON, MASSACHUSETTS

Copyright © 2020 by Vanessa Matic.

All rights reserved. No part of this book may be used or reproduced in any manner without written permission, except for brief quotations used in critical articles or reviews.

ISBN 978-0-578-70346-6

Tough Poets Press
Arlington, Massachusetts 02476
U.S.A.

www.toughpoets.com

I do not know what others look for
but poets look for this endless love, this
endless feeling that lives in eerie dreams.

V.M.

CONTENTS

Small Magic 7
7-11 9
Mutate Jesus 10
Bright 11
Everyone 15
Faded 16
Father Smile 19
Fear 20
Glitter 21
Golden Tragic 23
Humanity Is the Treason 24
Illuminations of Hell 27
Lacquer Copy 28
Limbs 31
Lorca 43
Metha 45
Oblivion 47
Old Money 49
Polo Lounge 50
Poor Blue 51
Pure Whiteout 55
Red Car Accident 57
Reflections 59
Rubber 62
Saline Sleep 63

Shipwreck to Mars	64
Sleep	70
Snubby	73
Social	74
Tall Skeleton	76
The Red of Your Blue Blood	79
Third Revolution	80
To Set the Sea in Wolves Teeth	82
Void Blue	84
Weedexit	86
Balthazar	88
Coke	90
Fem	91
Humor	92
Blues Are All the Same	93
Roller	94
So Quiet	95
F-Art	97
High Noon	98
Wake Up and Dream	100
War	101
Skin	102
About the Author	103
Acknowledgments	107

SMALL MAGIC

You're making a telephone call to someone who does not exist, if they pick up they exist. We all have a friend called Johnny and they are usually good for you. I made seven eggs and poured a tall glass of icy orange juice. I've walked through the city then left to the country side, nothing is too terrible to me. Sage trees, enigmas of your broken stomach a quiver of benzo erotic life lived in a suppression childhood of dark fairytales, life's longer pleasure of hiding yellow. Cremate me shoot me into space, you know they just scrape you out of existence and really who cares. I aim for ennui in this sleepless place filled with small magic.

I'm so bored I want a romance like Bonnie and Clyde, by the time I jump into this car I want to fall in love before I find out it's stolen. I want to do crimes with you, I want to find you under the tar sky snuffed under heaven, a moon in a spoon. To inhale life as if each breath is the last. Bite my neck to prove love exists. Speedy mini miles a moan for you I'm warning you such tenderness burns. Cold in the night you want to hold tight, flesh flowers disintegrate beneath your stare; across the room you watch me both of us touching not touching, watching the shadows of us move. I'm like a spider lily my back arches the jaggedness of my ribs as I lean, a flame of desire alone alone into your seeping kerosene lines. You don't look away and neither do I touching, not touching. Smear me across your paradise, across the drug floor of tantric punk rock. And are you jealous when you hold me tight thinking you won't win the fight I am a woman not a dream, the way you let me roam is for you made me into a fantasy. I want to be your driver put you in the passenger seat, drive you home when you drank yourself weak; you're so alone turn to stone an ego you build I can take the throne. Just let me in where I can sleep in your muslin gaze a nectar soft as me beneath your untamed laughter. Rare as flowers in your sunlight gallery a Pollock of wander worries you suffocate me in your madness chasing a high you cannot keep but oh if I touched you to suffer in this twilight within my skin of sonnets your eyes would dream things you cannot even see; delphic embodied into a prism of whims under red love. I'd cook you something you like and make you coffee in the mornings elucidating your pleasure dome an entrance into you burned out oblivion. You don't deserve my inhaled tenderness silk stars that move like tricky water. I'm filled with strange magic sigils uproot dawn, sex and death in the silhouettes . . . I wanted to corrupt you. As I always liked to be this drained on nothing but feeling you within me like a virus called love. And they said beauty didn't matter so come greet me with lilac under my eye, loose glitter and the sunrise in my heart with hopes of being the only lovers left alive.

7-11

As the light moves the darkness onto our skin;
There's no fear of death as we're aching to live.
We arrived in fire, breathing heaven; On our way
to buy a slushy at 7 eleven. Just two souls in a
wishin' well. Living in hell and no one could tell.

MUTATE JESUS

Pray for peace prepare for bloodshed.
He walked down the maple road, the
sunset was maple too and he was
far from home.

He stretched his mind a pylon of filth
from all the blood he lost in the sun.
Walking to solitude, till the sky was no
longer blue.

Freedom marched against the hills in
his every step. He, asexual venus boy
walking full of rage and hope, with no
rope to catch his fall.

He was magnificent like Jesus, sick, saved,
wasted in glory. Protesting everything for
his mutated flesh. Between the futbol games
and drinking booze, in between the social
fuse.

The horror of the world piled.
And he like a saint, a child.
Dead on the tracks.
Bless him well.

BRIGHT

Good music, making out, flying into universes, screens flashing like a whirlpool, screaming bats at the windows. That's hardcore you and I not pornography -ectomy every organ beyond belief. Immortality the veins in lust devoiced and love rejoiced. Was it a fading shadow on the red walls, the lights delicate like a first kiss. There was a splinter inside of me I thought it was blood poisoning or an awful dream, the kind of dream I had running from a demon that looked inside my eyes and said it was me. I might have not been sleeping, lip to lip a kiss is a slip.

A tapeworm to the love I used to hate, waiting by the bay you said you'd be there and we could be together again. A lie is a joke, I had to always try it . . . ending in a choke. Like the skyline crying. There were smiles in the sun and it got gray when the clouds marshmallow white dense the sky away. No need to close your eyes the gray subsides and yellow begins. In my own solitude no need for another white door, a room in your mind dark and unkind. We could get it on and get it on and get it done. Just like you told me. My hunger fades away and tricks stay the same, cloudy just keeps going. Invisible.

A magnetic trigger, one fireball set of eyes. I am ugly and still young. My legs dangle like two reckless snakes and I hate myself more. Then cloaking it all, a darkness in my soul like the clouds from above, as when you look down from the window of an airplane. How marvelous the seclusion, each delusion, contusion in my pale skin. Never sunburned anymore. The confusion is all illusions like the back of your head and they've kept on talking that night. At some shitty gallery, made to sparkle from some constructive light. Kept talking about you like you weren't all alright.

Early in the morning . . . a very first break, sugar spun honey. I can't remember you've changed. You could do as I do walking in the half distorted room, our furniture pieces we confused to show us a way. Piled papers, filed papers, and changed our days. You said you could stay in the same dream. I asked you that before we started to really speak. I had to laugh and cry so many times. Parallax the journey, and got a broken road, it was in my head a memory. From that time we drove Texas to Vegas. Wow, and got lost by some old gas station it was all white and green full of envy full of failed warnings. The calcified looking doors, where the earth stood still and sound of a highway from a slight distance demanded rides.

Oh well, each ride was worth it. Each one, even the failed ones. Johnny, Cash only . . . rides on Elvis gold steel scene. I was waiting lonely but the blue moon too called me, America was on fire a twisted cold desert heat. Remembering the people's faces in the small towns, they know each face and they watch your face like the stranger you are. You can get cold coffee, or you could ask for warm. The chickens golden fried like the sunshine with fries. We should drift forever. Live freedom, in the land of the free born inside of me.

There's always a silence not demanding anything. A break of ultra violence, shadowing non-retro America rural land. The dove milk sky that turns silk pink. Pastel acres echo, like Floyd. I wanted to remember each color like from a photograph in my scared mind, a natural born killer on the opposite side. Is it heaven yet? A neon supermarket and the micro gashapon machines waiting for change. And the milk gallon red and white. Fire sparklers New Hampshire and the young scream. Driving everlasting a last night on earth type of deal and it was so beautiful the French quarter of New Orleans all Spanish reddened.

Tee shirts and jean, teenage wet dreams, and beauty queens. Land of milk and honey, and here comes the money. Mary baby Jane, Jesus and the pain. A crisp air the kind like fresh cut grass. Rainbows after rain, holding hands like reckless lovers always dancing to confessions avoiding Church morals and tradition. Keeping the saint alive; A suicide high, with a belt around the neck seeing heaven; And then I put out the Christmas lights before it was even winter, they shimmered in summer to tell me . . .

Christmas is coming, there's going to be a mass. Chocolate in foil, snow somewhere. My mind a bee swamp and I am damp like a swamp thing. As I figured the fortunes we've had. A tank of dandelions with their stems swimming a stream of blood from morning, a light, and no one makes me close my eyes then the caving. Brings in a craving where you're hungry on full and full on empty. You shouldn't wait on the seasons and celebrations to make you feel good, just feel good when you want to. Like walking down an empty street with no idiots around roaming till you forget the silence feels just as loud. A mere camouflage of street corners thoughts flow in them, watching their reflections like an answer waiting for a reply, but the earth is too high to say if you should try. So just survive.

I hate to think you wouldn't try, it's all relatively too easy. After all this excess is a mere fiction of happiness. The objects blatantly changing. There our gravegraced bones sheer tones of love and misfunctions. If we were so strong it could belong. A smile comes like wind and all must be love then. You blew through me like a ghost, dancing in your madness knowing we could not stay in the same dream I held you closer than death. Consume me.

Clandestine each touch, a pallet of paint dried before my eyes. In waiting to be touched deeper than my skin. I burn off all color I become illusive, I am like the scar under the electronic you play. This too much touching in my mind and heart I let it disintegrate inside the night filled up with dim blue lights with freckles of red like a canvas. That pacified my madness by each dial. Remembering your harbinger poses as we ate with our friends and we were friends too. I kind of despised you for wanting and waiting on more. It was an omen in itself. A gated dark house, a ladder, a black cat I stroked crossing the road. Yet I was tumescent as a child with a toy. Moving how animals move, assuage.

EVERYONE

And if we made it in hell anywhere will do now. Silvers of the moon reflect in your eyes, you drink your booze on a red floor, wearing a cowboy hat, and telling me where to sit, more so pushing me into that place you need me to be; While you're rattled as I wish to taste you whole you're devoured by the sun. I close my eyes and think of weeping lovers that separated like us into sonnets of fire before anything at all. No innocence, in this permanence what once was love is a deceiving ghost I feel so tense shattering delicateness under my lust. I have no remorse I ride you like a horse into the illusions till you become a distant memory I do it to everyone, I do it to even me.

FADED

The heart can take a lot of sadness. There is beauty in the tar of hell; in the streets of homelessness of Los Angeles to the concrete heat of bodies and coldness of New York. I am awake but I am too proud for love; I would drown for love. While the romance of death circles like a raven against the high tower of my heart that has flooded a thousand dreams disintegrate in obscure madness.

We wanted to make out in the photobooth, and keep these images like a scarce religion in the pockets of our wallets. Maybe technology chased that dream away and we were empty kings on neon thrones bathed in the lights of absent people; The softness of sex and drugs pressing into the illusions of the skin that moves like violence. That violence which becomes erotic escape.

My darkness searches for it in the creases of people's perceptions; It is vacant, a sour light as alcohol spreading its venomed kiss. A tiny life is such a big life. The business of people is like the business of bees, each to its own tempo. Make more money, you'll be free. Don't look at things you might not like, find only flowers; But they too bloom in hell and smell of the sweetest perfume. Some happy melancholy chasing us outside. We have to go outside. We're burning up inside.

I take off my body and leave it in the mirror of people's eyes. How many flames have made me immortal to rage? How many heavens have fallen to walk in my hell. Millions come and go; People and cash; a currency of make-believe, almost. I touch you like a wet dream, gently on the wall. As all the dancing devils tangle my nights. There's another party, and another one, and another. My friend said come out, it's gonna be cool, V. A bunch of photographers, skateboarders, and musicians. I was bored of the faces they all began to look distorted like me.

I've never been bad enough to be bad. I've never known myself to be good enough to be good. In another world, maybe I'd have a body made of golden light. No one would see me, I'd be so bright. Is that what angels are like? Now everyone is moving like broken puppets slit into the silhouettes, I get so soulless trying to talk to the strangers inside of people I know. They see and touch, but rarely the soul.

Delicately this humming bird sings beneath the wing of my heart but it is too dark in here. And the drinks pile up like the hours, always the same. The instinct of my solidarity slithers down like a python between the darkness of people's touching. I exorcise my demons with a kiss, it ripples like a scar on a usb disk. The crowds they keep cumming like some sort of mellow erotic layer of magazine filth, and it all seems like some tabloid read. If only's. Love. Hate. War. Religion. Guns. Whore politics, changing dresses.

Ah but this warmth crawls under the eloquent cool of blood, the iris pool in my pupil. Where do you end? I begin, such a storm inside your desert. It's too late to look away, and there is no water. Drink me. Nightmares of youth collecting and cluttering. Terrifying silliness with our slipping hands. We wanted to be free of the previous revolutions. You chased me down the streets. I dared to look away. Yet what is more youth than the feeling of love?

FATHER SMILE

We speak of unimportant things too often, the death of love blooms over the sky—I close my eyes thinking of you, pieces of no-whereness fill me; a cup of hot coffee spilling over. Rooms transgress in mysterious daze that which is sorrow flies into infinite possibilities of all emotions rendered under a blue sky, in that which I am my father, my mother, a part of heaven, a god, a fallen star I've dreamt of weeping on the earth and while I weep it shakes this world inside me as if it is the only one that's real.

FEAR

There's someone dressed in my skin moving it's not me I'm not even here, you kiss me I feel nothing. You kiss anyone to feel anything angry at me I'm sorry I don't feel anything each step you make is an extra nothing. Flesh falling in sedative feeling I'm getting off tonight from the bright lights I'm captured by noise and sound you let out a sigh, no one hates you, even the people that love you hate you ... say the reflections whimpering in glass of riots made in this ether and fire. Are you happy? Knowing something inside you calls for someone else and I'm not sorry you are scared of falling in love for I placed a fear in you.

GLITTER

He gave me a book it was a realism of what he was like, gruesome—perhaps his demeanor was as a child waiting to be consumed but playing to win. Not sure what the prize will be, or what it means to him maybe nothing; a gaze of pale eyes I see every time I think I love him again— He seemed to think he's figured me out yet says something like "well that's what other people think but not me," it's fair to say it is easy to see the first layer off of anybody. Sure, I say sure to myself and him, I assure you I am no angel but love is obedient, lust is the stranger that walks in all romance so cheek to cheek hold closer the blood it arises in a parting dance. Yet I am as you see me pure, broken under your ether lights of your red floors where a kiss smashes stars under counterfeiter love. Here quietly waiting your arousal in a shipwreck to Mars, and are you coming with me. Thoughts are always braver than us, I've become to hold dear their soliciting nature. Did he really want me to read this book for he thought me cruel, or the world, inside of the book a man murders wondrous things perhaps the way it is written they are certain feelings of savagery, imagination, decadence, arousal. I think of him in his house he is amused by heavy things, perhaps some sorts of ideal wars where after he'd live thru them he would be happy—perhaps. Yet he is filled with cruelty to break something more fragile than he and when he believes he has done it he in his laughter weeps these tears which he eats that taste as snow in his living room, a nowhere home, a home not wholly owned as most others in this place of supermarket love and plastic, men sharpening their armor, women pasting their faces, everyone is extra animated so beautiful in a sense that it is ugly. I want to burn all my clothes keep only the basics, get rid of the glitter. I want to be in this bed nude, never to go out in trend I want to be here where we fill the white walls with noise. Perhaps if you are what you think you are we can drive very far, far away where there will be so very little to do, just us two. Then we can find out what we really are.

GOLDEN TRAGIC

And he said get in the picture as well as the flashes of the camera blinded me, this vacant blindness of white noise I could not even fall asleep in but inside this coma-tose blues I laughed so viciously, four men, five men, drowning into my sorrows with lilac curve which swells into the madness of the lithe solitudes that reflect on people's faces in alcohol and cocaine dreams. Where my heart is louder than blackness it rings like industrial disease, like punk Berlin noise that heroin Los Angeles white blown. And I spread into the wall sprawled out like a figure of China white paper-thin and my veins protrude a delicate flower; veins they purple and blue scope me like photograph filters. Nothing warms the body right now I'm shaking in the sun filled with its golden tragic. You know we're poorly loving, I cut myself asunder a piece of you that dies like me. Death is a faith we're chasing, but nothing more with all the dead stars that scream like fame wiped on piss floors. I no longer move like people I move like music and we both know its innocent violence.

HUMANITY IS THE TREASON

Still as the last sight or last sigh of high hopes there is a debt of the fear from our tears. The sugar of our salt sea where all emerged to never reveal thine own worst enemy, a mirror too distant to see; Afar ahead. I want to immerse myself in your heavenly body. Everything that is you, an eternal faint heart murmurs; To find what lovers read inside of fairytale constellations. A bird on milk white trees, sigils, third eye demise, demisexual spite, sedative lies. The birch trees in blue summers, the attic of the suns lips.

Towards innocence the feet quilt in the sand. The hands dread into the air touching what cannot be caught. We met disaster, we chased love; If we only we knew how to keep our minds unshattered from all nightmares that dilute ones demeanor. It is no longer a sacrificial host, it is the black spider in the thick web always waiting for the fly to arrive. Our hearts do not belong to us they belong to the terrifying nature. They are carried to the end and are worshiped by the salt sea full of tears, for all time is a masterpiece falling apart. Beautiful and dark.

There is a time when your whole being is a heart. Your body is a heart it starts from the bottom, then inside the stomach, it goes to the chest, it is all a heart, a fetus of imagination. The brain does not know logic and the arms and legs have no purpose but to carry the heart through life, for as long as it endures emotion. And the heart it consumes love and pain, its sadness and happiness; an embryo. It grows into the air, it greets the lights that shine and it echoes the voices from the depths of its abyss. They echo echo like a dead end, a neverending drum, an everlasting wind beneath the surface of all that is still.

Do not call for me, the earth is on fire I lick twice its desire. "If you do not chase your deepest impulse than you might lose your greatest desire." The nature repeats this to me in peace and asks me why all in my lewd head has broken in pieces such tiny ones I cannot sense the wrong or right or anything at all. It's because Seattle green-honey suckle trees, it's because peach haze of LA sun wet, it's because of black New York lit with streetlights of rainbows that glimmer in rain that sand away like flying flowers. Cruising past the graveyard of your opal mouth making a wish, a kiss of death enchants us. Obsolete where our bones meet, bones and more pile upon pile, roaming to the next house of bones cradling the mischief of life's beginnings.

You wish to love then begin, you wish to hate then begin, you wish to find then search, you wish to be lost then disappear. It is the ultimate truth to peel the illusion of uncertainty as we are in comatose blues swept by our ego to render a pure blue; Such as the sky in the certain clear light. I see angels dancing like madmen kissing your grave eyes, those eyes full of sea, full of not knowing any means; They arrive to their compassion set by the trembling wind. Humanity is the treason, the bones of our child. Utopia a direction to whatever end of the earth in a back yard of leaving or believing in similar to different truths. Stars pouring-in blood all over the ocean, where the soul goes to lay and you choose the devotion.

The bottom of the ocean, too deep for our thoughts filled with drugs, sex, politics, hysteria police, doom tv, skin for free on little screens, medicare on a soul lease. But you could still hold me if you can find me, keep walking through the hills of my mind, there we are ouroboros aligned. My heart full of mud and you reach inside of me finding heaven easily. Away from the sun, in with the moon of scars heading towards deep indigo Mars. I didn't mean to love you it's a strange thing to do, finding reasons to go mad is the best life to be had. The days just pass cut the umbilical cord, I fall from heaven's door. Tied up to the lips of the sun and my white tan lay on your suicidal love.

Indulge what heat has been faded and left I wanted to be raped heroin-e tied sweet, I wanted to be saved, embarrassed and played. No longer can I look at the speed the sarcastic elastic bittersweet. Compromises of hyper reality built our seconds in capsules our parents have not felt. And they said with their fists in the air. Humanity was the treason! Humanity was the treason!

ILLUMINATIONS OF HELL

"All the familiarities of my ex heart felt romanticism dated dumb witches that didn't know witchcraft like I" said the sorceress with two beheaded harlots laughing blood on her marbled floor. I had a dream that there was a killer in an Italian village who abused a girl and then murdered her by tying her to a cross and sinking her into the bottom of the ocean diving down to watch her death before she sunk too far he could not go further. Dreams lived in silvered houses we saw melting into the iridescent night, you married me with blood I said yes. Some people are sad because you're happy. Life is like a mass, sometimes if you believe in the wrong people they will turn your truths into lies. Friends are all fallen angels easily they can play tricks remember kings and queens were made by falling heads even family wasn't safe. How far have we really come? I dreamed a hundred dreams in this one day, I cannot breath it almost feels amazing this lack of oxygen causing the brain to shutter. Illuminations of hell cease friction of love. The anger of discarded children in toxic waste mother mother Bloody Mary, on knees of hyper reality and caveman ecstasy. Mankind rewinds, technology exceeded and shows our facades to be failing like politics and sex.

LACQUER COPY

Alchemist I laid out all your gods as ideas. Fear, love, hate, violence, happiness, richness, and further on. Paper cut shadows nearer your almost-sleep; A synthesis of a backward togetherness, postmodern suffered sunrises that burn down your dreams. A golden hiss that glows onto your bones, once more you are sacred. Once more you belong to the nature. And has the magic of his fiction reflected onto mine, are we nearer to fading stars. Currents in mirabelle lips, they shake like reason. Within music all seems to pour now, in this whiteness. Strange as death, elegant as youth. His love a nectar of a daylily, his pulse; Roseate in this quietness, he moves so gently I feel each whim like a magnet. How this once-warm sulfur risen moon shatters against the oaks and skins of all which surrounds us. My teeth grow, I want to bite each one's skin, I want to be one with everything. And the perfumed corridors like apricot musk tether against the oil paintings that rip open like ripened fruits in soft flame, my eyes conform their surrealism. It is much like love, all that surrounds us. Our madness a pure rush, a blood we taste in arousal. Love comes violently as hate. A swan-down of souls all living as one, and I touch him like the universe. My mouth closer to you, we kiss moist as the dew onto the now dark purple flowers, and they fade into this dark water, me. And you are milk that pours like the silvers of the moon that gray-blue the horizon. Sea-laced breasts, just pearls of softness, smoother, and calmer each of the caresses.

Under a dress, like racing horses, racing wild beauties, and the knees that from beneath you reach their higher silks. Into the lanyards of your disguise, bend me backwards for bittersweet tenderness.

Let it shame me like warm rain, and down drops each melody from the body like kisses; Dancing into vapor. Those kisses we once imagined in the dark, spoke of as supernatural gifts that belonged to the gods. How extravagant pain can be. Simple. Intrusive. Yet, loving. You once said you dreamed me a honey-made fish, no one would eat in the sea, but each man was hunting for me. You said forms of love are not to hold which ones are best. Impermissible, lewd, and stressed. There I lay like a dissected mermaid my bones chalked madreselva white, my body scaled like tasty metals, my breasts from thy middle split, honeysuckle blood. Has my mind become transparent love. This charmed face wrapped in moth wings, for your presence takes me apart. These new days that seem like tampered nightmares, at times belong to nothing but fairytales. And if I was to see you I'd gouge out your eyes, turn you around, kick you down, and run so quickly you would never find me again, my love. Yet, my eyes fall like cut diamonds, and they are swollen scallops crying in their own bath-salt, endless water. They redden, they close, await for the pain. Again, like a curse this benevolence between us. In the low quarreled semi-vehemence I played this gazelle, carrying ghosts in envelopes. Letting them loose by the blue-beaded towns, that drown at night and begin in mid-morning. The breaking stars that fade like angels, it is almost end of heat. There's this tranquil coldness, and once you lick your teeth the grains of sugar dissolve like your memories. Where you seem to have a photo that had been lodged on a shelf, sacral platted with some half-artifacts of togetherness. Not imagining ever perfectly enough, for there is no such thing honest. They mused us this way, an atlas of further realms. And he was my serpentine crawling like milkweeds towards me. Till the neck of love seemed to tilt as if cut in half. The other half was not there to lean against. Yet caper like tupelo, his throat an abyss, played like metals his body, ravaged with immortal depravity. A kiss that weeps like stolen tears, when you cannot cry for lacquer death. I wondered if I could see you now, how warmth would feel. Then I imagined myself a plant such as a sunflower, and you beside me hiding from the sun's fiery tears. And my tongue bursts red like its flames, and I still long for you. Is it that which you see, my eyes opal, that remind you of this world, that tastes like faith; soft as my heart that unfolds its mended petals. I am innocent, there is this softness compressed into each shape. I hear all sounds magnify under a film of water that I float through, the tears I cannot un-cry for new tomorrows. They will salt-ice my lips with their drops, fresh from suffering. All that is new again, will never belong to the past. I promise you so much more than those ghosts that bathe in shadows. To eat my own heart again, much as you have believed a woman could. There is this nameless birth from death, it uproots all pain. Incognito. All life is a separate dream, that attached onto another, and gave up on itself. Began once again as another self.

LIMBS

Desire, letters to nowhere...

To the nameless maps inside of me. There are three thousand tears streaming, a man cries very little. A leap of faith, a thief that is a starlight dance, many moons that grew closer to the ground; Heavy as our troubles, bright as our hopes. I stepped three steps back when I was scared it felt like I was sinking, good luck said the dreams as I watched them blur like sailing paintings down the neon streets. You left your records, your anger in a fishbowl tilting on a carousel. How many times will it turn till it shatters, are we just kids running around searching for fireflies? I don't see them around here anymore but I catch a glimpse in your eyes that fill with dark magic, with a film liquid pure in kerosene. How many miles do I walk to be next to you, an eye for an eye walking blue. I am an angel dressed in your light you can send me to hell into your darkest blood night my spine is made of hopes each column there is a note for you to read if you think I am lying, each note you take I'll break a little more but you won't see me shed faith I'll become more stubborn. I outlined the sky and ripped the blackness into pale, and called out your name said you're mine in a vein. And it throbs back like oceans in lips that say lovers are meant to die together, even you cannot outrun the dead end of a used up world playing the same record till the last drop, the pin exits, we are sheer. You still belong to no one else. There is a tree of pain, it carries love my half sleep afraid dreaming don't give it up for me give it up on speed.

Perfect beauty belongs to you and me, in eternal summer, and the winter in your eyes. I kiss you for all the reasons I believe our wounds will be healed, we fight with passion and no remorse. Don't mind much on what people see of you, but what you make and feel yourself is most indestructible. Fear is simple, validation is illusive. We live in the violence of flesh screens and the data of people whom we think make us stronger is nothing but electric friction, do sheep dream? I don't know; all my life I've walked away from the masses all my life has been a storm of destruction and lust, tied to travel and love. You will not find me weeping anymore to glow like your phone; Come to me darker, we know where is home. I'm learning to be numb again take away the ocean but we open a vein, now I'm learning to follow again; twice the devotion now we feel the same. Now I'm learning to show you rain take a chance and feel the pain. Every moment till we drown the same but you know me there is no shame. How I see your eyes they're dark again I go there, I'm so far away; heart to heart we sing the same. We waste our time in silhouettes I trace memories but I do not regret. Count the black in the lace we share, count the stars in your hair. What is magic if it fades in a splinter of a dawn burlesque arcade you know well I am your flame. And the restlessness scattered like sex pressed to the myth of pain. And the sad words, the defeated lovers' letters hung up onto the trees like christmas lights that were broken and could not shine. There was this loneliness that seemed like happiness, a too weary to care deal. Fucked by life properly till everything became innocent; My plane took off before I could reach it, for I waited for you at jet blue. With this rose that tattered like red silk onto the cooling ground. Everyone is waiting for something Casablanca dreams that are too busy. Maybe you were waiting for me smoking and playing chess, and perhaps I did not say I miss you. Maybe that was all that we needed to hear but we pressed our lips and shut our eyes, and went back to a terrible sleep.

The petals of flames fall like your eyes escaping into new dreams. The utter fear, ultimate stupidity. And then we will peel back our eyes like a corvette and speed ahead into an empty highway. There are no colors but the subtle signs reflecting light. It's brighter cold fingers warming blue say I love her, but passing kings leave lonely crowns they come closer to the end. No one wins wars, they shed blood; a million things will get you down, all the black you own is not deep as the night. I fall like platinum your helium laughter; you chase after one hundred dreams that shatter like metal, all your heart, threads of pedals. I comb out silvers, and now I'm ugly as the streets, I walked so many miles countless hours till I became dirt. As I dreamed of the ocean and you were not coming with me, I was only sleeping. To break down the shore a heart full of gold. We live in such violence it is the drug of choice to distort our solitudes further a realm of unreal, a realm of blood beaten by our own insides that have been cut out. Autism frail shaped, melted candles in delirium flowers, music spreads like chaos friction, we find books are not for free but no one reads. My headache rings rebirth, poverty, power. To trace you like I could hold on to forevers those that seem to outrun me. Police cuffs and salt shakes, bugs in spoons, bags of accessories pertain suicide; the marble slug in of our eyes. Life's like a movie, it's raining again. Your hands around my neck deep breath blackout regret. Let us make a bet Russian roulette and we get set. To sit in the stories of others and score, smoke money, smoke. I've become a corpse of flowers laughing at the hours, to trace all the ways I said I do while you played a fool. I would have to be so very high to feel the real that is only a lie. And that is high. For how far can you walk till you see no one but you and me? I do not want to be those people who do everything separately, life seems too short for such things. You were in the creases of my mind, like in the creases of my journals. You were an invincible force, an invisible man. If your darkness holds no light then you're not lucifer only one of the people in hell. To pull the stars down to the bay of your body. These light angels with dark eyes surround me. We stood in silences unknown by words, the world took turns in its flirting with death. I threw stones at the crows. I said hold them closer till there's nothing left. With a row of roses by a silhouette. A pack of cigarettes and your sweeter breath, it's as if heaven has spilled all its delicateness into hell. A dream inside dreams where feelings swell, the charcoal stones, and the blue line in the sky. As the yellowing moon turns into silvers. I walked 100 miles to the mouth of water. And I cupped a drink in my hand over my mouth, it tasted like your lips. You must've tasted me like this. I imagined you into a kiss. Began to believe heaven was you inside of me. Yet there are no faces just ghosts, and the memory of your fingers through my hair. Once the night devoured me I still miss the fire inside of you it's almost as angry as me. You said you'd kiss it forever if it makes me happy. And I loved him so much he became me, I loved him like myself, and more. Each thought became a dream and we lived in it, we devoured it, we became it, simple as loving, simple as laying in bed next to one another, with only this happiness that no one could understand if they did not live it.

Since when did you get in debt with society, we were a bunch of outcasts holding hands with the night punching out the lights. I woke up around 4:45 AM we were driving around Grand Canyon, don't bring your guns out around here. The dust of the pastel sun lit up all around the black vultures. I had a thirst cured by the cold beer and coke. We joked about love, sex, and politics. You were driving like a madman around the curves, trying to outrun the darkness as the sunrise was coming like a ball of fire towards the neverending road. Your eyes gleaming like a demon, we had to get breakfast at the diner. So we headed to El Tovar, I told you some old jokes about Bill Clinton. We got out of the car like two wobbling snakes, my insides felt like liquid lava. When I walked in everyone's head was gone, bitten off by my appetite and suddenly their heads turned to animals and they kept eating. I sat down like a criminal my head shifting down, my shoulders peaking up. The waitress came over, I began my large order of a rainforest coffee, espresso, fresh pressed grapefruit juice, honey smoked salmon with toasted whole wheat bagel & herb cream cheese, a belgian waffle, and the house made banana bread french toast. I asked for some extra maple syrup. And there you sat with your cowboy hat, and your gold chain hanging off of your neck like a monster, sweetly anticipating the next plan. I directed your attention to the woman with fried blonde hair, wearing an ultra pink get up. She went outside with a plate of leftovers and proceeded to feed her white pitbull. I started taking photos with my old polaroid camera, I actually got a good one of her and the dog humping her leg. You said "Where do you wanna go after this freakshow?" in this low tone that was clear as the crystal-like glass that echoed from the left side, as the waitress was taking away plates and glasses. I sat reflecting the sun, the shimmer of wet glass in my eyes; dazzled by the man who just cleaned the windows. "I want to go to the desert botanical garden, then maybe bar smith or rhythm room, I don't care I just want to finish the paintings from last night, and shoot the final visuals." My slurring speech piled onto of the food being brought over. There was only one more day left that we'd stay here, I decided I'd stay up till I was so tired that it hurt being alive. We held this long straw across from one another as if we were holding hands. And the clanging noises that surrounded us filled the atmosphere, everything has music to it. Even the sun. What do all the cowards do when they only have selfishness to offer, discount on vapor? Well tears are only superstitions as is money, we follow a flow. Now that we know it's all a myth but one is still currency. A private world is an exhibition, frankness nothing more. Candid as the naivety. I don't know why the quality of life is not more accessible, people work so hard for merely anything but dreams. And this life is short, shorter than there is true love. If I had ever felt that true love, well I would surely let it kill me. For materials mean not much to me. But they don't let us see the beauty. Originality is illusions of things already created; At the end we're all just gonna rot and die the same. In retrospect don't lease your soul to strangers. I no longer remember the sun it's been mid-day since holiday; Like a cocaine salt shaker has been poured all over the sky it is lined with nothing but bright, distorted pale gray. It comes in gulps, consuming the surroundings. I felt I was only 17, wearing a simple dress; My hair in a mess, this body tangling like flower chains. I set the christmas tree on fire, I let the light stay till spring. It's like walking on a street that took all your kisses, swept them in the dark for other lovers to recover their happiness and sorrows. A creation of speed to destroy. Youth spent on materialism of plastic, as one moment recycled plastic becomes sweat.

I had began to withstand so much I could not know what it was that I was looking for, the crows by the window, the tears on your face; And a name I know, I began to mistake. I want to fall inside you but will you wait for me? The clock does not turn back, the ocean does not stop, I am tangled in a secret kiss; how I am pulled here; dead in a grave, adrift and lost where you tattoo over my name. Soft as you, face and face next to bloom, how sadly the music plays and fills my lungs you would not know. My friends I lose, nothing I choose but splinters to put in my veins that's where my heart remains. Such things are a curse, and the sky aligns in your eyes that are paler now than this pastel blue; This quiet blue that looks dirty, such as the emptiness across the streets and the sweet the corners of Los Feliz, and Malibu grain and the bad parts of Hollywood, the highways, and the nature that comes before you come into this place. I starve myself for your love, I know I am not welcome. I am like a stranger that overstayed, and brought you a foreign present you kept because it reminded you of something that you wished for but could not keep for you lost all your heart inside the alleys you believe are hell and they are nothing, only mere gamble games. You let yourself loose like a street dog and I understand. I do not pretend to be hurt, my throat filled with silence. I will not answer you when we separate, we will glow further away, if you see me . . . we will not be there. As you said you once you believed in this something, this art lust, this haunting hurt that stabs you when you are alone, you lied. Maybe she just wanted something bad to happen. Talking to strangers, believing in the softness of romance and rage in the fixation of death carried inside love. What a touch can make you lose, true reality. Religion is like sex, dirty invocation that becomes pure after confession. All life, wrapped in garbage romantically inclined tragically declined. It's easy to say you want to make love, it's hard to make believe love but the flames burn like blossoms in kerosene; And tears are regrets we waste to forget. We laid down in the hotel I poured the rose petals that he gave me on the graveyard of his beautiful body. And the gold in his hair, with the blue in your eye. The sweetness of ice and fire; A moonchild with a prism in your mind. Love is a death that's to come, and reemerge; I dress myself in your desire open your mouth to taste a fire. A reflex in your body that you cannot control. While you read me all the literature from the library in your soul. A stream floweret imbibed into one another as we glow, like two snakes shaking closely waiting for the snow. Stealthily in your body I roam, come now don't come alone.

I heard they said I crashed the black '69 dodge, tossed the motorcycle into the beach, did some writing on the top of the stone mountains where I was shooting; That what sounded like the best music I've heard in years. While the noise mixed with ravens and then went missing . . . now I'm here. I got arrested in looney town, 200 black and yellow snakes biting one another's tails and making love shaking like the winter had arrived. In my mind a thousand realities and surrealism fill like starlight they glow when ignited in the skin. Eternity is subconsciousness and that which we make from a piece of our self that is carried into the world as a ghost of love. What is eternity? Art, love, our multitude of connections and mind and spirit. What is it to create a thing that is a form of life beyond our bodies. Eternity is our neverending spirit, perhaps our creation to form what we no longer possess when death comes. Reality itself seems like a disbelief in eternity by the way things disappear, nature is violent so is human nature. Yet what is destroyed is recreated in a cycle, eternity still exists all living matter continues to better and for worse. The ability for our insanities where we do not control what is reality is a further realm of contradiction into what is it that we truly believe or know? What do we exit and come into anew, a soul? As the whole world is a maze that moves like a billion images that do not stay still, they move like electric currents. How deep is the sea, eternity flows like ether and sound. It is all around us. Our childish manifestos that do not make sense, what is it to concern oneself with psychology or science. I do not exist in the idea of religion, social status, or much of anything than our eternal being which can create a beauty even if distorted. What happened to our spirits, fragments of us tied to the birth we give to life and artistic fragility, things that linger onto memories like time that we erase as if sedated by our non-presence. We lapse amnesia angles with no crowns but our memoria that travels with stories like history with lies. Eternity is in our design, a phenomena of nature. To be as human as possible. Closer to the nature. Free. Without hate. With only this breeding love that makes all things grow.

Just drown me there with my hands in your hair. The second time I noticed him, was at the perch bar he looked quieter than everyone else; later on I found out he wasn't. So I never knew what it was I liked in the first place. Watercolor sensation, this mellow-eroticism of pained lovers beaten by regrets of city silhouettes. The fumes of smoke piled like clouds as they carried my mind away; Inside the soul of the music that played between us. How much longer will I suffer the unequal friction on my skin that flexes back the muscle till it cannot repeat. Wanting to be a baby in his arms, in the world of scars. As politics ripped off gloss-like magazine filth. There were so many surrounding me that it became like a silent aquarium. Stop touching me, beneath the skin is the soul it cannot grow whole in these crowds dancing near me. I could not dream, incandescent; he was a memory. That meant fiction, by now I can recreate us. Icebox smiles left from spilled drinks, disorganized hearts disguised by being grown up enough to love yet immortally paralyzed. I was only a child, loving only what I could wrap around me, they said that was all so foolish. I started to believe them. Masturbating shimmer, like the stars that fade by day. All escapes us as I seem to put one foot sideways instead of forward. Wobbling over my own duplicity, when all I've dreamt of was the simplicity of flesh. But it mounted to my lips like a dying flower and I need so much more than its wet death. For frenzy hands that we've ignored. Your fingers down my throat like a serpentine, you coil now; As I would flex onto your every movement. A vespertine of touching that avalanche of passion which indulges beyond the skin, scarring burns out; Was it love completely mistaken. I want to smile with you and leave the stars to die in the throat of glass sadness that fills all the hollowed people which we do not see as we are reaching higher ground. To go so far to show you how close you really are. When you miss everyone it means nothing at all, interwet-high-gloss, hologram-orgasm. Trashy is likable, good stuff is intolerable. I put a little smut in my coffee for the morning to go faster. "Everybody. Every Body. No body. Some body. Somebody. Nobody." breathes back all things consumed. All my wounds in the sun, and then I change in its pain I'm an angel just for the rain; Till the night begins and all sadness roams I become evil once more.

If you can touch heaven it's near hell's gate, sharp as desire that chases pain. I'm insane. And the sky lit up with infinite music, swelling with kisses and tears left buried in the wind. And the scent of your skin filled the earth, and I breathed in so deeply my lungs began to feel as helium balloons that would send me off into space. And I wished to be taken far far away from here, I would leave a letter wrapped in gold thread and rose; The echo of your laughter would be muffled into the night as a deep lilac wine would drown into the darkness where all lost souls wander into nothingness that nothing which becomes so fragile we don't believe we can exit. I want to die beside you, is that love? Eyes filled with vacant truth but you're not listening. So who's the lover now, I wipe my life away by your voice and your body that now seems fading into a photo I remember seemed like love on a needle pushing into my skin until I dim I reach for him, and in my sin I swallow a pin. For ever wanting to taste what pain was in the madness of our rush where we opium heal our scars, conceal truths in dark rooms, and we pray for rain. I try to erase myself out of your memory, and I believe I do it well. Finally, maybe you hate me and maybe you take me; A bad high, leave me in suicide, the walls talk rubber-flesh they whisper what we did, touch your body and feel the void, a careless rapture from within and I cry for you and

I cry for my limbs. Life is mostly lonely. There is not often love as there is loneliness. Its serenity a dead end to repeat all the cycle that society bound. To be hip like that, to have jeans like that, to have the house, and car like that. And why I am so ugly now is because I had once given my soul on lease. It is time that seems so vast until a year slips like candy lava under the tongue. And you have licked its tears that made heaven drown in the tar of liquid dreams you lined up by the city skyscrapers and the distant lights; That now seemed like your heart, fading slowly. What premises but fear, and hands that seem to slippery to hold. Hands that never meant anything at all. I will stab you with terrible love.

LORCA

Los Angeles the poetic poverty you live like a romantic violent, a termite of mass hysteria erotic dreams. Everything in one man a Cadillac deal to painting and roofing, to junk and junkies. Art, La Cienega, swamp thing, love thing. Envious of the only letter and record left was kept by you. Playing mysteriously to me.

And I really miss you jail bird blue I think you died and fell into the fool. Alcohol is like a stain in the sky that strains your eyes and I realize I am you and you are I, I'm not yours but you are mine. Infinite sound, infinite time to discover the buttery stars that align in dreams I whisper inside of you.

I bend like music, handcuff a breath that will not last seduced by melody a thing of the past. I'm not haunted by ghosts for I've become one running around this town till faceless we met on a night of noise and fire; Immortally yours, your vampire. Lorca your Spanish eyes sing with dark love and I make no promise I am not from above.

A blood wedding for my veins while silhouettes melt bondage and chains, a sweat of love lives in trust you let go and I know I must. Exiled, alone we were destined to explode. There is always been this stolen excitement to celebrate the assassination in the capacity of feelings worried about sin. We made sugar out of salt. And the earth is but a stone, color and bone, marrow and whole.

We sing deep songs when the night is long, you pick the flowers you carry to my room. The sadness of song is akin, fascism is everywhere. I've become asexual, jealous as all lovers, jealous like your criticism. So I've made a shitty film your voice appears. New York seems terrible, cold as gold rivers of wall street with death overflowing. Suicide, and death with greatness a spectacle. Love me like death is coming. I sense its urgency in all beautiful things that faint like the night. Skin is like young live flowers and we inhale soul, I'm teaching you all I've ever known. To love without remorse.

METHA

Pissing on the reeperbahn, sex-media life-show, girls crying in front of neon with deteriorating looks boys say is fashionable.

Crawling into the black limo. The palm trees scattered all along the highway tossing their long leaves in the air. They are like golden vultures towering around the city, all around it. Platonically syncing a dubious romance; To live and die in LA. A psychological damage, paraphilic paradise dusted in romantic gesture of poetry.

(it's like you never wanted to forget each moment you were alone that you really weren't alone at all)

Undressed in butter stars soft skin that moves like tricky water, your blood perfumed view . . . innocence chased to destruction. Synesthesia covers wet night I'd follow you down darker.

Methadream, war workers, coffee, and the scent of colder air under energy shocks. Ether and candy and cooking magic. I was sitting alone with everyone and the noise was filling the smoke. Love under sunglasses burnt out under brightness.

(love is like a movie so kiss me while you're bleeding)

100 books and 100 more align the sky of the walls burning in

your eyes "I hope all history burns" tears become madness, they're too much love, they're too much feeling. Once again you bleed trying to smile accepting life's complete.

(love is a nuclear war)

Did you get busted for waking nightmares and drugs? / Turpentine alley and guns and booze and laughs, cast out into the garden of evil, Angeles / Summer heat is like paradise lost in music praying within dreams that shatter in sins / You're so cool, cherry rush in Ginsberg Gatsby blur beautiful America / Noise and pastel serpentine, whiteness opal sunshine and all love divine.

(Lonesomeness carried into the howling night, obscures kisses left in chance. Another one-man dance, shadows on walls that sing heart echoing songs.)

OBVLIVION

Virginal marble, silk golden string, Chanel 5, there in the midst of favoring the ocean of people under the influence and you under the heroin watching with fisheyed vision. And the magazines and shit and technology and manipulation. Color stream like wild rivers diving visions merging in one. Screens fluorescent laser drag and interwet dreams.

My arms longer my dreams stronger . . . Aching for the morning to catch the dreams that have fallen off as sleep awakens. A new day breathing, a beating heart that reels the sound, the vision, the breeze like under ether. The oblivion a burning black hole, escaping life. Like a dark dream that never goes anywhere but inside the storm, as the skin that touch where we're mental. And all the flowers torn like limbs in a fever burning, the religion a pylon of filth.

I have learned, loved, and laughed. After twenty years where am I? But a living dead vessel. Nowhere further to go, but I keep going much further than they allowed . . . And what does he think of me? If he thinks of me at all? A mother, a wife, a sister, a whore, a lost friend that fell behind his back. As our ways parted directions that were most unlikely to rekindle as you reached towards them with deep longing.

The story never quite is complete, we forget to remember it is like a memory waiting for the touch to be remembered again or completely forgotten by what we meant to taint the moments falling. The day was rain you sit down and cry. I was listening to the moonlight touch you and the noises blue came through. Your Fugazi record tearing your heart in two. Wasn't I the one who said I loved you. The time kept slipping station to station. I wanted my records back.

Well so, death is not the end, that's what Dylan said so we must be pretending for a happy ending. Comely we dance a new vision efflorescence soften the violence I've had too many times. As daddy would tell me to be wise, and not depend on other guys. We're all somewhere else now, my name is Carnival I get down to the sound. I see all of the clowns. Poor crazies I thought they were all free running in the streets half vegetable, half human, mutated magnificent fools sparkled in gold dust.

I wonder if some people miss you and don't tell you, and the time passes with you not knowing that they missed you and you might have felt the same if they just said the words. "I miss you." Sometimes you've got to walk through all of the rain and then you might forget your tears are falling. And then you keep on walking. Brood attractive pity filmy dissembled and we are bittersweet. Our words belong to forgery subjected to illusion when in each, reality is a reality previously handed and used. And I still think of your misshapen edges as beauty, and you still bruise easy and dream big.

OLD MONEY

Encircled within this light in a strange darkness of marmalade tears. I skip past this photo of an engagement ring you showed to my mother with a red ruby, the night is calm, warm, delectable. I stayed up so late writing and when I was at the party in Texas I hopped of the jet, money ringing in the mansion, old money, I left everyone and kept writing, they were getting angry at me. I moved further into some language of darkness, it's strange to know that people we knew become strangers, like a certain special bouquet of flowers that fade, and while everyone was busy I was filled with noise and fire. I thought of this you, this you I no longer knew. I thought of love, love I tried to give to another while in my confusion of corrupted thoughts; the kind that make you leave in mornings even if you don't want to. And then I think of water, endless, breathless, small us, barely touching in this universe that whispers . . . you never knowing how to open. Me shutting away like shutterbug eyes seeing in pictures that spell away into magic which cast into my skin, never to stay.

POLO LOUNGE

I hope they don't hear me. Do they hear me? Over times, applauded for no reason yet I'm a human fly. Beverly Hills hotel a 1940's ether dream. No words form I foam at the mouth as photographers nail me to the wall with ether. Kosher Colombian cocaine, American dreams, sinus screwed, and boom buggies in syrup. And I kneel into a limo to save me. A cocaine salt shaker that his sister lines with a black credit card and the gold on it lines the stars in the room; how decent the indecency. No troubles but the delays, be careful don't scratch the paint. With a 400 mph mind, responsible and un-captive, go swimming. Eat lies like you're in Burger King, all is sunlit even the night. True grit. Only God did the evil, and you said you didn't believe it but the sunshine acid said it did.

POOR BLUE

Pool poor blue with the smell of candy canes and clorox, there's been three fights in the last two weeks. Music crying like the death of people, chanting people, money fool prophets, colorful ideas of lingerie. The 2 dollar ice cream, melting like dreams in the sunshine. Pastel blues that fill the sky and return you to diluted love again, perhaps everyone forgot to keep their minds, and they all trash each other. Lately all I do is worry, interesting hours paper cut moons and moods; seven bruises like planets. Lonesomeness we tender flower carry in car music lightness, all over America. My resolutions are never new, Black Canyon hollowness, beauty in serene, Colorado color my dreams.

Meet me in the pine sparks, then meet me on the East. The empty skies that lay like indigo lilies, acres of plain lands that golden-beige solitude, I think I wanted to free myself and become a worker, poets have no money, no fame, poets are sitting in chance rooms like laughing flowers telling bad jokes to themselves and anyone who listens, and they say everything is paid with love. But where is it? Nightingale zodiacs, death that smells like a burnt wish, lithium crushed anxieties, parasitic paradise with sugary coated miseries. I am experimenting with your bird drugs, wholesome poison. Everything is political they say, everything is like a religion, a hell of poets that became ideas. And my mental state riding on the back of a cockroach silver-lined, gentleman-like with dirt. An interwet vacancy of surrendering, a whole new nakedness.

Does it mean we pay in elctro-currencies now. Will you laugh when your cats dies alabaster colorlessness, love is a nuclear war in my light concussion I walk ghastly in the rudeness of the sidewalks. Everyone was a young hustler unemotionally deranged and exclusively illusive. Vague as open-stretched heart gates, penis-drawings, and crushes. Short circuit-control, hide your eyes when you dream, one more bullet that is now tangled into guitar strings against a red canvas. Yahay yage romantic murder, I point my fingers into the ceiling but I am laying face down and ass up. The difference between coolnessness, who are you branded glassy-eyed, pope-dope; five blocks and scoring. Heroin to alcohol, always take the first shot and you won't die. Glamorous products, things that say buy or you will be sick; another migraine press conference junk that spanks you like a baby.

I am addicted to kiss, hooked on something. Money is like toilet paper but you need to wipe your ass, life on a toilet seat. Harsh lungs now, a whole life lived in flames. Methadone-drone shooting blood paintings, you never sleep anymore your handguns snubby we shake like snakes in a bed you are loaded as it. A silencer I wanted to keep for the silence of sleep, and memory of trees, that brush like fairytales. Let me reach in for the poison. Everyone likes the bang. Everyone likes the bang. Rage fascination and love's assassination. I who have forgotten to love have became empty as them. Uproot my madness once again, blood in my veins to sing in refrain for I wish not to lose the innocence in me, flower blooming arousal-erotic bezno-nite. Flood through me like melody, death wears longing strange fruit from sun clouds. Eerie green that says all envy what dances so freely and those poets they curse their pain that is existence of brave. I gathered a bed of white orchids, silken like your body before bathing in absent desire.

Your teeth broken tiles, scars that run deeper than gold mines, I mined paradise out of your eyes. Serpentine kiss of Valentine, one fuck memories to solitary dancers that weep with star-ridden lights which cut fears into illusions and keep dreamers sane. But I have given my name to become another, twice born I learned to not know what is faith. My hand inside the ice bucket of the clouds beneath your heart. Under the pink rose of the heat I devoured the ice of your solitary fixation; that was the high in me when I could no longer cry or sleep. Music-organs that breathe back magic still distort us like we are open, and the largeness of strangeness will devour our longing forcefully violent as nature. And I am skinless haunted by the wind that howls, breathes like love, pain and love. Love and pain.

Nobody can talk you out of using, nobody . . . life's a killer, maybe you'll swallow gasoline. It could be at any time these urges come back, we substitute feelys with some strange religion. My gay priest said there's nowhere one can go, a sorry state. We seem to be always sick and he says "Are you holding" well I got nothing, just company an art work of flowers. We end up walking knowing old neighborhoods, rocking rehabs, dead friends, just tattoo hours of lovers on high o'clock noon benzo-erotic. Hassle shakers, with guns through a donut hole. My face fallen off my bones into the two sunny side up eggs, pastel blues say I love you like a slap in the face. Put on your good shoes and own up baby, I do I'm an asshole and so are you.

Systematically right wingers drug hysteria police problem solutions. Philosopher prophets that turned our nightmares into songs, black cats I collected from rainy street corners of Los Angeles alleyways. They said poets were bad news, but you never read the paper? Ha drill some more holes, drag jobs, rent money, leather coats that say you guys are still punk logic. Forevers are so long, street life romance no regular no chance. Nada, but crazy to say we can spend nights like kings. Because now we gotta go, "I wish I could win you back" says the sweet one sharpening knives for a living. Saddened by passing hours and flowers in Korean restaurant windows. We walk like old people when broken down, worn out like "god bless you my son may you go to heaven." I look up at the sky stars filing the blackness of unkept promises. Superstitions are real. Keep me alive. Super high.

PURE WHITEOUT

Ravaged and raged in beauty within these sage trees. Embedded flowers in a photo album and lamented all fear aside in a cabinet you convened. It was simplicity still, between the fever and fury of bee swamped aggressions. You like an old friend sitting on the balcony above the wooden stair the blue painted gasping the skies face, opal. Knucklebones all felt out of breath and secret, kept only to hurt myself over and over. Ablaze solitude where it is flourishing tonight in Connecticut. Orchards thereby looming and grasshoppers singing songs we heard before.

I've hired a demon, a beekeeper, a gazer of bull fights for hearts we mended in cruel summer freight-less romancing. I put my slippers on walking between being doomed and loved. A woman of roaming against each heated night cooling in the misfortunes we bent like steamed wood to create good or shelter. The mirror water, air's cleared and bright light in the darkest day. Twelve stars shine and all like gold pieces melt into your eyes, the eyes sliding their own compassions . . .

Unfamiliar is each ending, and we held hands below the twilight. A mischief of country games, I could climb that tree and the forest will show me all of its colors and leaves. A birthday present resurrecting childhood, the moments of mischief; Scrapes and bruises we had in fun and quarrels. From distance a dog barking as the rain is starting to flourish the green, like our eyes putting out the fire with kerosene. The flatlands of simplicity palm handed smoothly touch the jagged everlasting hills.

We scooped the night to slaughter in the day and with that my worry. Crossing the small bridge dropping inside of it a swollen velvet kiss. It was last summer we spoke of shame, it was this summer we spoke of pain. And believe me it is better to speak of pain it is more honest. Whom bares much regrets after all. With the frost that makes the leaves break the pain is unfrozen later never-minding, growing again. He smiled full of previous scars. Nude, abased with wanting the growth waiting for light like flowers.

Standing looking at one another there was a great silence and the darkness was eating viciously at our treats. Saying youth is fading, a new kiss steadily crawls like insects, I feel like one of them. Later in a photograph I found of what must have been us, blurred faces with detailed laughter beneath a summer shade. It was the last I remember leaving this place with our delusions in the split milk, pure whiteout.

RED CAR ACCIDENT

The accident has accidentally taken off more than just giving scars. The seatbelt whips and slips. Your ghost vaporized in the air hovering to watch the impact, wax body hanging. It's because I am a sad girl it's because I am a bad girl, Jesus, Jesus, God, Mary. My red racing cars red racing blood drops in midnight to dawn, bruises seem long ago. A girl you use to know well she was not me, not anymore. Fugitive grave nor reborn or afraid. A gambol of destruction we dance to, flesh is beauty. Penetration deep inside imbue the addictions left behind in a mental state and your foundation a new dare. Inured nervous system labyrinthine mind for the focus of your broken spine. Ten pillars keeping it together, metal hook fish, little worms, column of protection. Against odds no harbinger to tell you lies. Gossamer in your vision did they already make alterations and incisions. All put on all sort of things that Holiday was probably on, overlapping colors in the cold room the sensation crisp aspirin and lemon washed. The stink of death an acre stretch across the stretchers. The high opulent, the brightness a darkness that is so stale, a blade harrowed bent blunt shaped jabbing in the deep ends of each tender position. Childlike watching a purple dinosaur smile at you; Eating the sunlight and you smile, the walls wobbling, faith rotating. I am a saint half living wholly floating, marble floor twist serpent tongue lick the feet walking barefoot onto cold tiles in fire icy hades to remember sensation. To see the medical attention with head doused in flames walking by you like candles.

REFLECTIONS

Is it summer everything is filled with lights and breeze. Even the darkness, it is smiling cheekily with noise in the wind and beauty in its danger. So vast is the black night, it is not a monster at all. As I thought when I was a child. It is committing itself without resisting, it is happy and excited as the daylight. Monsters are the people we meet, only. Playfully committing all sorts of barbaric behavior.

I once glanced this face in the mirror, this face horrid in the mirror. Staring at me telling me how monstrous I was and that I had a mouth full of serpents, eyes drained of water, gray blooms growing in my hair. I almost screamed oh the horror, And eyes so dead as no oxygen passed, not in days. Slapping myself in my cheeks gently only enough to redden, back inside efface myself within attention.

That night the horror did me grand failure. Full of scare, shouting dancers. The men and women like howling dogs; and I was a shy baboon. Nor was I trembling but I began to drink, the kind of time one has when afraid I assume. Sheer love, voluptuous fright and in drink delight. I was no longer whom I appeared. They too were a different crowd and they dazzled like stars blurred by fog. Warm the walls and colors dark in this decadent place. Moving like cut-paper shadows they dance and embrace. Oh no again the horror from ghost stories we shadow puppet played. I drank once more, once more with rage.

Someone gave me something that night not just the worm inside some whiskey aged cargo ship of 30 years ago. I could hear them breathe. All smiling hooks crooked and all swinging in the boat. I was so tense could they see? Who would care in the picture show, if tomorrow there were pictures at all. Whatever I see in front of me I swallow I drown immediately. Love and hate await here. Not for cruelty, only truth if it came on the opposite door shamelessly joking.

And I drank to the stars and the people and the bad and good times. I closed my eyes weak, and sharp, a woman beyond belief. Touching my skin with completely cold hands and so dry as the cold morning wind. They pumped me, they took out everything. Here in the white room, white white white and sheets and all. They made me give my life back to this hollowed body, full of useless aim. Now shadows in the lights with stethoscopes hanging look like little demons. Why frail body have you let them exhaust us so?

How things solidify intolerable carved craved pain red blooms to blue feverous concerns on what the body is maggot off. Who are they that have dismembered us, crippling our touch to the dark. We seemed all night to sleep. Not to awaken in a bed full of chalk skin. In paper nightgowns with an ass hanging. Magnify my nakedness as if in a stubborn museum, a statue almost lifeless. Footless you must pretend wait in the bed. Sacrifice unto me stillborn openeth the beast in bread body. I have given from myself not all I can. Bread body pulled in pieces, legs drape. Eaten the bread body whole and raw almost born in edge of wilderness of pillared clouds that cloaked the fire by night. Before all of the people came to addict each one, another to save the body. The bread of tomorrow. Am I? Delicate. Strong. Embodied.

Morrow you horrid creatures all like locusts in a field of aspirin crushed smell and morphine will cling to the bread. Evil is before you a sin of forgiving myself for the shadows have lost their final breath. Coasts of grievous locusts prevail like a veil over head in my slumber from the night I put under. All pocking needles in such places and darkened was the sun when I arose like a rose waiting for blood on its petal, like water. Put a Hebrew death star in my hair for I feel so frail. I must have walked Egypt in a cold stare, three sound pyramids. Like oracles stretching rods inside. Am I brought by the south wind here to the cold north. And shall I cover my face in snow like earth covers its face in night.

RUBBER

Consciousness is a phantom of speaking into, a corruption of understanding a world inside that is a rule of nature unique as a flower made of birds. You envied me because I believed there was something more than parties. As you rotted into the meditation of your disabled feelings it is a party come it is not meant to be enjoyed. A horrible luxury to be primitive is in fact indulgent, I desire so little and so much. The words that I have are all made with music, the kisses that I might share can echo into your soul. You only have to be able to follow and surrender. Surrender like you are walking into the blackest deepest unknown and all of your desires are strong enough to consume you with a blanket of such tranquil darkness where you will feel only the complete reflection of your soul. In this moment your design and desire will open inside-out to consume everything else. You are luminescent a dark angel, lucifer. You and I. No world but what is inside. With only this certain creation that comes from pure existence. What is it we use, the last high? What is re-addictive, love; Which seems to morphine through junk. But what of kiss? And filth. And music, fascinatingly screwed. There's no such thing as pure reality. I bought you a screaming rubber chicken to prove my point.

SALINE SLEEP

Rozz Williams posters and Slash magazine, France and romance saline sleep. Louis Céline in a tear. S&M and all that jazz artistically declined sub porno erotic. Shaking hands in parties flattering instagram friends with cute like fancies. Intact with about 20k fake followers given to photographers and magazines alike and skin trade on venmo. To dance in desires aching for a love with no return. Sometimes when you are very quiet you can hear everyone's lies. If you drill a hole inside of your head the right way you will have a permanent high. If you wrong the precision there will be repercussion, we live for our addictions they haunt us with beauty they are destructive as they are kind. A permanent high we chase to feel alive to feel pure bliss is to feel nothingness.

SHIPWRECK TO MARS

Altair I see this last grave like heart
Struck in ambers of the cooling flesh
of mine you held against your irregular
body You were mine for sometime

There's always been a line keeping us
together like an isthmus Yet hope is
like a clue always changing And we open
our crippled hearts in the cemented and dark
dream

You are beautiful even in fatigue I pick flowers
Carried to your lithe violet red eyes now from
tears I scattered among the star tendon sky

Light lurks into the world like a firefly wailing
down the foamy joy washed into the sea I
no longer dream as a snake ate all what's real
You were Adam and I was Eve between all greed

Or some part of you and me
That seems like such a long
time ago

Now ...

I can offer nothing but the deep kisses and the touch
of a warm hot flame to your body That turns cold when
you no longer know what you feel is real Glints in the
milk red skin I flicked in a soft pain in deceit for the heat
escapes And when have I slept along the shore all my
dreams got carried away What could await me but a late
bait of soaked bright color Death was choosing them
Not us my love If you could open your eyes and wake
up my love My love, the lonely places where we will
not find lonely again

Enter a light
Take my hand
If you ever
believed in me

Buried by the sun every day A memory of loss in your
heart I felt something so strange was arisen and it lifted
in the thin crisp air between the moment of happiness
and sadness A birth of there was no distance in this
moment A hot ripe peach like kiss I blush I mute in love
I cannot breath and it dissolves me I no longer crave for
you but for my peace this tension abides the emotions
green and red, feverous and envious Clench the shadows
if you could I run with them and you no longer could

For how have we ever loved My marbled eyes ravage under
the water for you cannot touch them now Only my mother
knows how to save her drowned daughter I cry for my selfish
ways Immure me for you will always do so Forbid the
incarcerate

loathing singular human imprisoned within beastly volatile times

The illusion of a girl you've loved is entirely a dream
Made of nothing but the ravage glass like mind . . . fragile
Amongst the worlds bitter structure of beauty and slender
pain Flexible honey sweetness almost sick to show him
each night he can drown against the dream of her lips
Worn out kiss and to the triangle of safety he can no longer
enter as he has parted from his magic and red red red
A flood of blood in my brain dilute into my heart crashing
the waves you obey and I tolerate your shape

A willowy body tangled in limbs of another to another
I never wanted another, you offered me the world To
the world with victory in your eyes and no longer did
I hold effortless grace in my limbs as you say that I
do Empowering the hollow like trance is a state of
defenseless aim I am not from the Venusian sky you
think of so beautifully but a fallen star from Mars

Grace like silkened beauty woven in my insides
Of a corpse like body subjected to death the death
of gravity Yet divinity is in the nothing I do seek
time to time to survive a cold fire to be alive
Christian martyrs poisonous eyes hung in the
air to contemplate the diminishing prestige of
crumbled history Death enters like a shipwreck
and piles upon on one the hands and skin

Loathing and fever fear

Shutter blind your love
Is it a persuasion I have
never cookie crumbled to
measure the crumbs to lick
the bittersweetness for it too
loathes and then lingers like a
planted demon seed inside the
body

We can not out run the nature nor love?
Can we out run love . . . A demon fleeting
and then standing touching his heart
In a universe he had arisen in the beast
of man the beast of burden and my sympathy
is in this creature Finger by finger and he is
beloved The night deliquescent preserved
The illuminated light over his frame and the
stars blooded in the white of my eyes Was
that the fire of no sleep or tears I do not
want to know the answers I do not seek

You use to feel for me without looking You'd
touch every part of me the lengthened longing
would show you the breathing petal like cords
in my neck, you would kiss The teeth in nerves
across your soft flesh closed into mine I became
an animal aching to be with you And hour by hour
still when you'll leave this skeleton and loose the
hands and voice of art, torn like ligaments from
the sky

It will dilute in empty air the earth will be smooth
silk and jagged like razors where it must be and
it will drift away These sensations like glory

Pale open hope the ivory, skin to skin bodies
Ground to ground and my belly your belly . . . raspberry
blood in spiral A classical tune of smoke like souring
lavender in the dissecting field I am the rose thorns
You're the lender dear I Brave now, that you found
something immaculate Have you? This dark dead night
answers her across rose fields, questions her
I wither in Januarys fine jewel like frigid fire you
have escaped and I claw the bare heart scraping
the joy for tomorrow, for tomorrow will no longer
cut slit into tomorrow clouds Full of blue smoke
in heavy lidded eyes like linen on your body heat
A faithless room becomes a room A musician
without a voice tonight but a guitar and strings
that play like a body Nightmare freckled songs
that linger to the bottom of your soul they have no
control Sunken, sink into the quick rapture

We do never out run the capture
It's blanket like light or darkness

I knelt upon my knees not to pray A cathedral
song parasite cream tongue on breast fills a
beautiful scream to the moon and silk space
nervous for fragile love no thickness cast the
due to death separates So does if we wait and
await unstable collections of the mind tumble

in whirl wind left secrets in the deep end

I believe in your spirit if doom it should lay
The angles and demons have all fallen down
here and they dance together So I believe and
I do Psalm hot rod heads to touch you while a
hummingbird blue sings in my finger tips to tease
you and a thousand moons weigh nothing

Divided constellations seek your faith in the
fever silver-thinning cancellation of the rippled
sea; a mouth you open to say "A saint, is awake"
And to look at me and pray You knelt upon your
knees to the savage waterbody of a woman you
see with a piano spine but I am that hunchback
do not look at me, I am a broken song and you
long for me

SLEEP

I don't want to leave, not now without this dubious romance. Gunpowder blue, I dance in your velvet room filled with venom while nights fill me up as I feel like I am dying. If you called me I would be on the other end jazz chords playing like my heart beat. I love you but I can't say how long, we live in this strange abyss of times people think they need all these materials why? Afraid the skin translucent as interwet 20 second beliefs. There's a bell that's ringing it might not be anyone, and I'm dizzy do you care, so show me. There's no bottom not even in a thousand feet isn't that strange? Next month I'll be gone maybe Spanish Harlem or if you know me good even further after that, I could show you true music true sorrow, do you ever feel a heartbeat in the palm of someones hand. I left a memory of tears under dried flowers on a grave of some poetic landmark of history I came back to see blossoms, hummingbirds that sang new songs each day, even people are not civilized so. You know out in this open where there is so little people it is something special, chickens and cats noises and much remembrance of the city, guitar players that come into this nothingness because all music belongs to no one. Strangers will tell you you're beautiful, you're pretty, and they might be looking for the dead, or that blues show in the only bar in town. You walk out of someone's life you might be free, or a rainy day just for you felt this certain way. Taboo of blue, feels that creep on you like a hat superstition I am a writer, in your skin I find new news, I have drank too much tonight and blindly I consume this thought of you after a pill I took to feel this thru I called you at least in my mind and we spoke. I said I liked it when you pushed me in the corner trying to undo me pushing buttons that you could never push as much as I could if I would let you this moment full of nothingness. Filled with the magic of the city, suicide of Tom Wait whispers and cowboy songs that swell sweetly in my heart a primal scream with a slap from my own hand in my face. A bonfire with noise and rattlesnakes, I puke I'm poisoned but for some reason I am even more clean dong rituals bloody in scintilla sands an orgasm to the wind which sets to sea in me. My eyes burn, my heart empty as yours in this fear, rage, panic, I want to make trouble with you but where are you? Chicken. In thought of putting me in that corner and nothing more. How boring. I cancel my plans because everything bores me like this till I silently disappear. My head hurts this moment pounding drinking water to drown me, my body drown me, crushed aspirin blue bed, jazz filled room noise of neon bloom, I smell like a wet rose crushed into the smoke of a lavender floor embodied in opium under your tongue, light eyes caressed by strangeness, thrill me more. Once more with tragic. You know no bounds of my love, erotic as the melancholic night or ravaged as the suspicious monstrous greed to devour you. Come to this place of nothingness, where everything exists, even this bliss sweeter than what you have ever felt . . . deviously swept into erotic asphyxiation of your mini miles that run into data data I do not believe in anymore which is super human, with little joy. I pass the time in such prestigious places that when I see the tents I get so crushed to know many must be there in any moment, after those times I swan at Chateau and got drunk in oblivion not to the capacity but to the extent of me ordering sushi in the suite from another overpriced place. Singing songs to the piano guy, hallelujah jeff buckley and radiohead I'm a creep and he says "Wow that's beautiful come back tomorrow I'm playing again." I hear tap dancing outside don't know why, the wind is heavier, scream shrill, I can't sleep I can never sleep I am never calm. I feel so sick I spit on the floor, it's the spit that's clean that perv would like to lick up. This stranger says "You must have a husband I'll tell your daddy you need someone to keep you safe company" I say "I'll manage" Washing machines noises in my head, I can rip off my own shirt these tiny fragile girl hands that become mean. Dogs bite your knees, growls I hear make you bleed, somethings sometimes we don't feel. I just need some real sleep. I'll be real. Epiphany.

SNUBBY

No one cums... broker dreams, nostalgic sickness, heavy lips, ember weeping... stars pulled up from dust bugs that needle thread into your tardiness see-thru like illusions flames... you'd shoot anyone to play victim. All your friends watched the apples burst. Bugs dying gun metal clean transfigured body that sexuality becomes alien. Strange dive bars, methadone twilight where pain is one thousand characters deep in sleep. A ticket you bought but couldn't catch the train, you'd involve anyone in smut, the snubby hit custody. Bloody traces like a saint scar skinned and sinned alive, trading skin like a murderer. You say you want every feel good and you still don't feel good. What's nasty I provide you pure gram and pound. I know the innocence of sleep and how you kiss me when I am sleeping. Still this outsider lurks on the sleeves of darker friction changing your song to death. I have designed us genius gods, but they cut heads off immortals and everyone's blood is sacred. Everyone is god, they all have laughter like stars and what are eyes now if not watching the shooting ones fall and draw blood of our servants. You use to spit tales and reap souls. Strange magic entering a mouth of the abyss, only one witch burns. I am at the cross waiting for the fire.

SOCIAL

Socially unacceptable people make great lovers. There is a tree of pain, it carries love my half sleep afraid, dreaming. Don't give it up for me give it up on speed. Everyone was a young hustler. We are told not to give away our art for free but we are minority artists at times not of wealthy cause, and before we can put it anywhere we might be dead. And the world might be dust, and we might never know if we touched someone from a distance, art is to make love with a stranger. How do we create this love if we are suppressed by gallery and its friends? Art is a reoccurring currency of dreams, it can be recycled so the limit to earn from already done works from the artists is countless if allowed. They say make your art bigger and sell, bigger canvas, bigger photo, bigger poetry. Yet just because something is magnificent in size does not make it magnificent in its nature. "All the familiarities of my ex heart felt romanticism dated dumb witches that didn't know witchcraft like I" said the sorceress with two beheaded harlots laughing blood on her marbled floor. I am living in an age where we are a currency of make believe. I am not a woman but a dream, you forget that I feel. Your platinum helium laughter undressed in silk stars that scar by mid morning when we've laid out like lovers in beds where we pressed likes to like another and our data stored on to someone else's superstitious, mysterious skin I drown in. Anxiety of what it is to be romantic now, buzz sounds of coffee, white noise, coke, dreams, devouring sleep that is in silence. We all know it's far driving half an hour in this town and I come from the west, my eyes greener because I do love you. And some people say they don't believe in soulmates because they've never felt true love. And maybe it will never come or maybe all the likes will be downloaded to turn into some new device where 100,000 likes equal a love. I guess that's why I never wanted to give others that admiration, you know all our friends disappear anyway. And so does all of this.

TALL SKELETON

Naturalistic was the invisibility of you
Transparent mouths that hold seance
You spoke that your sister vomits fire
Seven realms of color animism shiny
or dry, a contrast of wet visuality I sleep
as I dance, I am so tired

You scheme lineage of religion made
under your name within refiner fire,
babalon desire into a darkness; A
divine sign, a star inside your mind
I do not continue to wait while you
sing

Breathe back the sea, which is clearer
in the night to me I lose myself in after
waves that sail me to a different place
Your voice so silent under a shell crushed
eyes face me under a collapsing moon
where sorrow is permitted

You burn simple materials as you deeply
lay, dense in the colors you wear made
of light I hold you close to me one of
your faces staring, a fright delighting

me ... coming inside within the lavender
tar air cluttering a taunting warmth

There is nothing new under the sun
It will rain I will show you how to
whisper I will show you how to bleed
I will paint your eyes with black kajal
Down a wild valley your soul wept
A silhouette you wrote such a happy
song I believed every child will smile

A blossom growing more and more
Near my bosom beneath the floor
Lust to seduce, to charm, to mend
I hear you crying carrying a candle
once again; There I teach you swift
arrow cast into heart to tear through
the dangers of the night

Sweetly you sleep in lullaby moans
that save a little lonely boy he is an
angel walks towards the east; Heavily
bodies demand always greed pale
hand under flaming flowers that make
girls bewildered hearts and lungs divine
run in obscurity

I find you've traveled brought back to me
Again, again in swollen sea a lithe violet
melody; Kissed by the heat your opal
mouth, sadness so moist holy and mystic

rejoice when innocence is little and lost
Smelling the fear is vain a mating of angles
all imposing deep

I leave this place I bring gifts and I bring
something back to home; Tameless
virgin viewed bestow a lick under
emerald eyes round and round the
tiger spies; Slender, naked, personified
Under a red lens magnified

THE RED OF YOUR BLUE BLOOD

Our tongues flicker like magnets; Liquid skin vibrating. I wanted to sleep with him, forever. I cut vertical into the throat of a bird it is the last song of the humming blue. Everyone is permanently bored and busy at the same time. The clouds roll like cotton candy down into the hills, with six sided stars falling. It's summer, the heat is like sweetness of arousal carried by the violence of bees; Into your reflecting skin filled by presence of backward love. All tears are simply a treasure of nothing's. Many times we sat in silence watching for the light in us that never shown. You were the boy that let me put aqua eyeshadow on his lids, and paint his nails red. There was so much rage around us, from the screens, media, sex, and youth. As we shut the world out with our desires. We walked the streets like saints, half awake. You bought me a wedding ring, we were nearly 21. Believing that Vegas would set us free. A pastel suit for you, a see-thru white dress for me.

THIRD REVOLUTION

A new invention of blue, you walked through snort snotty empty reel streets. Your insides in turbulence, so much blue everything becomes colorless, the shutter of your lips that have pretend kisses.

Metha-drone bodied, rap-punk echo-psychotic with money outlined cheap accessories, with our comical politics. One hand on crotch thrusting into popcorn comedies, I like the "bad music" it's not overproduced, I like the vintage, I like the curiosity that has been lost tranquilized by sedates conscience where riots are just false profusion.

War is very real, sensibility wankers are very real. I don't want you to like me I want you to think I'm everything you've ever hated because it's parts of yourself you hated, self sufficient to disturbed realism. Overpriced housing and art painted like candy, glamorous and faded after a few licks like the cheap dates that cost too much. Because all you lied to one another bout passion.

Aah I have no more eyes left today. I immerse myself in infinite intensity and the volume raises high and low, low and high. I think you hired your enemies to stop us from being fascinating, did your idols become too much to romanticize. Scared of new Ginsberg, scared of new Crass, new Plath, Babalon consumed ideology of easy. Stick sheep together to say bah bah, another runway of narcotic plastic.

Lifeless images that bought your mind plagued by death. Oh but we both know snakes rattle at night and the passionate ones will keep hissing executing loveless trusts.

Heaven in America; TV, skin, wasp, heels, metal, illuminate the shock society repulsive as your urgency.

In the time of peace there is chaos; We love animals we hunt humans there is chemical danger, there is violence. Echoing hearts breaking and history smashed like stars.

Can we replicate our senses? When there are killer robots on the street there's no going back, drone weapons and simple desire satisfaction manufactured. Life in seconds, science fiction is reality and that what has once been fantasy is reason.

Implemented artificial intelligence, best artificial intelligence will achieve full control. Singular conscience. Law of history shaping futures. A lie that speaks truth, we are in awe of tender hysteria and an abyss of catastrophe collects into the data gathered amongst us till we priceless become endangered third revolution.

TO SET THE SEA IN WOLVES TEETH

I had a dream you stabbed me I'm constantly bleeding the strange thing was I wasn't mad, I still loved you.

I'm just tired of all the loneliness.

So I ran in the streets till I moved far far away from you, and I danced in bar rooms where I belonged to no one, I gave myself to the decadenceof desire, I changed myself the image you loved you began to despise.

You leave the room empty burning with love love off my skin.

If you do not see me I do not exist / I am a negative as if of film / I bleed into this surface but I do not go into place / this permanent death he says is nothingness.

A hollow summer . . .

We fall from the sky in a rage of our fears we open up and the world disappears.

My veins full of wild roses bleed with thorns you kiss me with fire and leave the stars.

Life's so short you lost me in a blink, I couldn't forgive myself if I loved you longer than this day and the carrying of this pain, a pack of wolves surround us.

They wait to eat us while we bleed, and my arms longer my dreams stronger; Still I reach for you my phantom limb and the burning of this loss makes me claw off my skin. I wonder what is beneath the red, the bone, alone. Just so alone.

I desire your scent that seeps into my skin like flowers I remembered beneath an ocean bed, discarding my clothes in the bloom of sunset; Your heart a darker friction I sink in the salt of tears till I am drowning. And I hoped you'd find me there where I am sinking, to hold my hand in the permanence.

You say you changed your mind when you believe you wanted somebody else, you said you changed your mind when you needed somebody else; And I was that piece of yourself that you didn't want to get rid of which you chased off into the streets with your coldness and bitterness, don't you know I've suffered this long only to lose.

But it's just the illusion of romance; you don't even see me. I'm dressed in your silhouette I want to enter your soul and its twilight like our last kiss; don't embrace me. Kiss me, hit me I know you want to I am parts of yourself you hate and love. I am parts of yourself you hate and love.

VOID BLUE

When I think of blue, I think of a bright blue old Cadillac car, blue sky, blue water, when I think of fire I imagine a child walking through a forest of flames inside a protective shell, I think of black and white, eyes like computer screens, flowers bright pastel like sunrises being devoured by green pastures or skyscrapers, infinite abstraction of logos, lips, hands, bodies, mirrors. Boxes, ornate, paint, photography. Beverages, their colors, textures. The feeling of red, the feeling of blue, the feeling of neon, books, paper, dvds, tables, vases, aloof trees, false eyelashes, anime. Liquid. Sex. Innocence. Animals embracing. The hunter being hunted. Heatwaves, sunsets, sunrises, danger, signs, Vegas, Texas, Colorado, California, New York. Far away, far. Architecture, stars, freckles. Loudness. Silence. Sadness. Hate. Love. Reflection. Bombs. Self destruction. Hunger. Obesity. Deprivation. Mirrors reflecting starlight that show scars in the ocean, birth of glow aligning fragments of unknown desire, danger. Folklores and horse rides in midnight sun. Some people rename themselves the name of a blue felt pen. Some people are schitzo. Some people are addicts, hooked on habits that transfix into surrealism they become godless gods. Some people are hope, they heal, wise as streets, time, stillness. Some are destroyers. Multitudes of kindness and evils. Heaven on a white plate, resembling food, hell in the street . . . a quiet homeless woman asking for honey the gesture makes you cry. Pain you've felt for coldness and cruelness. Physical strength, birth, blood, fighting. Toothless handsome strangeness. Tattoos, knives, dullness, dresses, suits, coffee cups, electronics, music gear, cords and wires. Acoustic kitty, orange, oranges, lemons. Prints on walls faded retro. Green, army. Authority, green and gray. Wall Street empty pin drops heard against futuristic hell. Dogs barking. County serene, sunflowers, ears. Tablecloth. Picnic baskets and cakes. Lavenderia and fog. Los Angeles in spring a cold night. Tattoos, cat on lap. Riots everywhere. Darkness in the skin so fair.

WEEDEXIT

Wait wait awhile says the ocean which made me sad, why would I go dance around with all this confusion which I have drunken myself into a tinsel sky creeping me out, and my back pain from twisting around funny at chateau last night; as all the so and so's came past me. I was sitting with a friend and then another friend comes up to me and says "I saw an angel sitting in white, who is that? Oh it's you I love you, I love you" she said and I said "I love you too" and we embraced as old friends do in vintage hallways with cigarettes. The night proceeded—heaven on a white plate, resembling food, hell in the street. So then today arrives—I went to the farmers market bought some overpriced whatever and mentholated cbd lotion, growing up America baby, weed governments now paced out on Kafka highs that will soon be legal too. I just got back here from Paris not too long ago it's been bout a week or something or something; for time seems to cease in these moments of togetherness or emptiness. Anyway it was very much like Los Angeles not the architecture just the nightlife so you have to switch it up maybe have sex on Rimbaud's grave or anything to keep away from those small circles I kept running away from in the first place. Oh but here I came in with a bottle of sex appeal wine, no really that's the name of it. I'm not joking poets are bad at that but we can talk about dark humor later we all know life is hot like that. And so there I was going out to see Bry but I couldn't believe in the city or nostalgia anymore

I was so down everyone seemed to be on heroin maybe I was wrong—but no one could look each other in the eyes anymore, hidden agendas are all over the place, even this place. Oh well. Soon you will shoot up something more exotic than even you thought possible, perhaps something animal, or nuclear yet to be synthesized by paranoia. Mutilation of constituted thought dubious exposure to what is law masturbating within a boredom of betrayal, but no one comes. I long to love or breathe; both seem like longer fingers dreaming of a tropical echo or mouths that eclipse just when I think we are getting closer we are barely touching—yet someone always gets fucked. I just squint my eyes. I'm a little blind, is that the exit door?

BALTHAZAR

That day they went to Balthazar for brunch. It wasn't as hot out as the other days, everyone was like an insect running around in the humidity; The sweetness of lovers and wet silk-gauze bodies glide all over the streets. It's always busy here during this time especially on Saturday. We could celebrate our happy last days from here to there. I've overheard this will be the most brutal winter yet, thankfully I'll be gone. If I wanted that kind of winter I'd go to Aspen and enjoy the snow. I'll come back here to visit, I travel so much anyway. But all my fashion friends are coming September, hey I'll miss them but I can always see them in Berlin or Paris. And here ... I fail to really like anyone, I mean to really like them. Too many roommates amongst friends; And you really might not agree with them, they're the extra wheel. No privacy. There's also no point in moving in together with some of these illusive ghosts that borderline being just a dick-nose anyway. The technology has exhausted much respect you could even possible grasp to have for someone. I've never taken anyone too seriously when I see them sprawled onto everyone's media. The same circle, again ... of men and women. I'm going so far out I don't think I'll come back to my self. But hey my ex never liked much of anything, I've always admired that. After all what are you liking a moving image, a parallel universe of a hologram world. To whisper is better into the ear if you have the chance of feel. And surely it's not that people don't deserve love/likes ... it's quite sweet we all support our friends but then you see some people that you know, you judge them there, and you see them out in the world, they're the same. A failure of likes. What a strange thing to think about when we seem not to over think things, there's less money in the world but too much to a 1%. While there's tons of high school kids growing up homeless. There's wars in this generation, there's this unequal presidential race, what does it all mean? It's like I'm watching idiocracy, it's playing in the background when I'm living. I'm just sick of the falseness in people, like chasing sex for a night. The tacky disco under their tongues, the bad beats, that skip heart beats and make robots out of us. Pessimistic isn't my nature, I know there are such lovely things and people, I've seen that beauty. Yet it is a mere fragment in this polluted realm burning the skin of lithe bodies in this fragile tension of chasing winds. Or maybe it is I just met a more larger amount of assholes, but I even pity them and give benefit of the doubt while keeping a 100 ft distance from the sort. If I want to see them they'll be out there on the media on everyone's page.

COKE

It was a few days ago I haven't spoke to any of my old friends but I saw one of the girlfriends she said she was in love with me and hated you. Then she went to the bathroom and sucked off a goat, the goat didn't want her she cried and came back home to you. And my friend with white leaves on his nose said we died in a dream kissed the glass filled with vodka speed and said he saw the sun. Then I bumped into Romeo and he was wearing a rose velvet suit he had crown of flowers in his teeth and he gave it to me. Stabbed himself said everything was obscene, I'm not Juliette so I threw the flowers like a bouquet a tranny caught the flower ring and started to sing. Violence was everywhere and I was dancing unafraid your evil was wanting me, and I'm sorry you will never get to know me.

FEM

Feminism doesn't mean sex with everyone because you're equal as a man, man sluts are a thing too. Lovers aren't shameful to have or those summer experiences that you'll remember when you're old and gray, but bad sex is bad. Like those guys that come on strong only to disappoint in every field even in bed not to mention romance. Leaving your underpits furry doesn't make you rebellious it's all bout what kind of grooming you prefer. Not being a bad person doesn't necessarily make you a good person either, there's a difference. And always remember the stories old people tell you are usually true and good advice. Also always remember in your mischief and fun, to love to truly love like no one's watching because they really aren't watching. Life's a moment, in one the waves are heavy the next they're calm.

HUMOR

From the balcony across he asks me if I live here or if I'm on vacation I tell him "My whole life's a vacation" he says I've been too quiet and I say "Maybe you should try it sometime" he laughs as if it was a joke. I'm on the balcony waiting for a bottle of wine, there's a view of a statue of an angel in the garden it's beginning to rain again, summer rain. I just sit there waiting to get soaked.

BLUES ARE ALL THE SAME

The blues are all the same, I truly love this whole album and his voice. And the simple poetry of lyrics that are perfect. Anyway the blues are all the same no matter where you go. I catch the most talented, interesting people with the blues, it is like we are chasing things that are fractions of what we really desire. And sure it is some sort of purpose to create what we consider art, but when we look and hear art there's so many forms of expression perhaps the greatest art is love. Perhaps the reason most are unhappy is because they have not yet perfected the imperfect art. For all our creations are a birth of another, an extension of ourselves when we give without selfishness. Perhaps we make it a song, perhaps we make it a painting, but it is always to sustain an impression in the eye of the beholder. Perhaps it is always some kind of affection to belong to another other than self as a ghost, a ghost of love.

ROLLER

Give me a rollercoaster death. Who wants to die in their sleep after all? If you ask me how I'd want to go out . . . old, listening to My Bloody Valentine on heroin, jumping off the tallest building in the city and before my fall a guillotine would split me in half.

SO QUIET

When she was quiet she was so quiet that all the people around her would become particles flying through space. There was such a stillness in her posture that it seemed only her heart was loud and it was louder than the noise of music or people. On this peculiar night she wore only red lipstick, and dressed in all black. Everything about her was sleek and tidy, her hair, her nails, her transfixed gaze. Emerald swallowtail her eyes seemed to fly like glitter, shimmering like distant dreams. Her hands were so delicate the wrist playfully with tininess, in fact she was quite small boned, bird boned and pale in fact on this very eve as the moon was full her skin would glow under it. It was if she wasn't meant for the dirt in any place, especially the crowds in the fields of art and fools. Yet she loved the glamour of death carried in all things brutal, sweet, innocent, even in those who would do anything to survive. She was drawn to the animalistic kingdom its simple pleasures. She had a smile I believe one that wasn't even really there, a half like phantom one. At times she was approached by a swarm of people excited to see her for no real reason it wasn't even her party. She would become disoriented and talkative, like an aggressive animal. One that felt shivers as if intruded on, people thought this was her being entertaining. And she was just the small gestures that would leap into grand ones were a small dance, graceful in this delicate violence. She would get bored and rush away to get a cranberry vodka, she would hide in some secluded corner looking at the strangeness of people. Sipping this bitter sweet drink she tasted as decadent youth, then as one would turn away she would disappear and you would imagine she was somewhere around but by then she was in a car looking at the ring on her finger, imagining the shininess of crystals and metal in all objects. The coldness of all heat, and in her imagination of clouds she would dig herself into her oversized bed and shut her eyes like she shut out the world.

F-ART

That one artist that took my poems and promised to do something magnificent with them when I didn't even ask. That is a thief I hate him, he disgusts me. A leech, a cockroach, scum on my shoe, I would stab you with life in the throat. My rage is even more perfect for no one asked for your petty self. You have not even come to be great as me, you look a fool. Pink blown and confused like the fumes you use, a splatter of paint. How dare you ask for words you can barely read, I want to throw you on the floor and use you as a mop; Your hair looks like one and your nose. I will sweep my living room with you, I will bloody it with the romance of hate.

HIGH NOON

I've arrived at noon my lover abandoned me, demon seed in the sun melting inside of me—a whole sea of man, of man beast is beloved at midnight sulfur he suffers his eyes transfixed by my silhouettes. Weep his eyes for his regrets satanama I have become catatonic—soon the doom will crawl under me, I'll be a cat in his nightmares, I'll be a bat with heavy wings, other repulsive things that seem sweet until they're not smiling. And now I smell of heavy blood wine in my mouth and full cherry flower on my skin to pale the angel I am dressed in yet there is only my skeleton history under this meat, peel under my benevolence and my mercy is evil within its restlessness. I tear him apart like a flower, he is reddening, arousal and fear look the same now. His skin whimpers and there he pours in the shadows his corpse hardening, music plays it is quiet; it is dusty in this place of forgotten tales cockroaches and lizards, rattlesnakes I use to catch there with him to make my belts and boots. He is so alone, maybe he'll die that way wishing for a ghost to come by naked pale as the first day he laid eyes on her with all the mystic delights showing glistening remorse on to such lovers whom exist in a realm of ultimate desire. Yet the fire is dying, he seems weaker by the days passing in his silences with others. The moon and stars collapse for sunlight, as I am possessed by the ultimate seduction—sweet angels die for my love I crush them like tar in a pallet of plastic, scum is the fragile and beauty the devil that time abandons. There are two doors we're walking in opposite directions do you see?

WAKE UP AND DREAM

I don't like waking up alone, if I'm leaving I hope you'd come and you said yes. While they were kicking their habit in the streets there was a room full of meat puppets trying to escape reality the ones half away/awake talking about politics while their women dance on someone else's lap. The room was cold and there's some of you that would shoot glue to get to death, somewhere someone says "you're my girl" to some girl somewhere and they proceed to be lovers, so the day breaks like that and before there was excess there was a few more thrills of people thinking for themselves. Lovers smoking in bed with nothing to do but be strung out like god.

WAR

And soon there will be war
And soon there will be plagues
And the walls will come falling down as lovers hold tightly to kisses
And love will be the only thing left to eat

SKIN

I've written it all, now the only pages that are left are our skin, delicate, dying, and with the final breath all my words will perish. It will be as if all the sorrow, romance, and love never existed. But oh how I dreamt you into wonderful stories, each one so decadent no time would erase such beauty.

ABOUT THE AUTHOR

I'm 100 years old my height is 5' 7½" my shoe size is 7/8 my measurements are 34/23/34 I have almost died three times. One was a car accident, one was an overdose, one was drowning. My favorite color is black, some of the most inspiring people to me are Rowland S. Howard, Sylvia Plath, David Lynch, amongst many many more. Some of my favorite stories are by Hans Christian Andersen. Some of my favorite movies are The Lovers on the Bridge, The Girl on the Bridge, Wild at Heart, The Island of Doctor Moreau, Cat People, The Little Prince, The Only Lovers Left Alive. I saw a pink ghost at age 7. I like to write poetry, I like to eat desserts, and I like to dance; and I love to be in love. I believe in love as an illusion of freedom in this world where everyone lives in 100 dreams in the same day. Till not even one is true. I believe in being fearless. I believe in unbreakable love. I believe the parody of celebrity and the contradiction of peace and war. I believe in our breaking hearts that fill all the glassy screens and parties when we are diluted friction. We are living contradiction. I adore my idols but I wish not to ever be as any of them. I like the story of Henry Darger, I like Chet Baker, Neruda, and Hunter S. Thompson, my favorite Ginsberg poem might be America. I don't mind working for something that I think is a possibility, I am a terrible liar. I am the best friend one could have I'll always be there if someone's true. I've met many important people, I've had dinner with Prince before his death. I love traveling, I've lived all over the world one of my favorite places was Berlin. I made my first poetry visuals and short movie there. I will also always remember Amsterdam and the time I made a custom burger in Burger King at night that was better than the ones here. I'll also remember the rain, the bikes, my face on the rooftop of the shoot for Zoo Magazine. I'll also remember Berlin the first time I came I felt so odd and so lonely everything looked so quiet I landed a big shoot for Tip Magazine and my billboard was all over town. I'll remember meeting Mudhoney backstage in my purple satin blouse while my bf said I was his wife and we were engaged. I'll remember NY and the '60s guitar I got, I'll remember the places the streets I kissed and loved and disappeared in tears with all over the world. I'll remember to never fear things I desire. I'll remember to let myself become all that is simple as the neck of a rose that breaks without remorse. I like expensive things like many people but I also don't need as much as I have. Happiness is my greatest goal, I feel I've been born blue since age 3 and my uncle that died in the former Yugoslavian war bought me a blue bear from a stand because the color to me was beautiful I still have it . . . it has a red polka dot bow. I'm Croatian. My father is a professor and worked in parliament when in his country . . . my mother studied as a lawyer. My mother has a weird heart, last year was weird for me. I saw lots of blood. When we see blood of people we love we understand nothing is forever at that moment more so then anything. I broke my nose about 6 times in my life. I have anxiety and insomnia, I don't take my problems out on others, knowing that each person has their own demons. I did ballet many years I'm still very flexible. When I was little I went to a party at a European president's house and fell in love with a little boy I would bring him cakes. I was only around 5 years old visiting for the first time. I was raised in Seattle. My hair is brown. I don't believe much in people but I try. And every time we talk about ourselves how much is still unknown. I'm the little house scorpion with a venomous acrobat of feelings born out of sand dunes and the apocalyptic romance between a spider lily and a crown of live thorns. I like to eat cakes, dance, and make poetry about romantic doom that lurks in the chaos of all lands.

ACKNOWLEDGMENTS

Profound thanks are extended to the following for their generous financial support which helped to defray some of this book's production costs:

Bulent and Olga Akman, Adrian Astur Alvarez, Apollo Staar Fine Art, E.R. Auld, Thomas Young Barmore Jr, Maxime Ballesteros, Dudgrick Bevins, BloodyKnucklesArt, Gina Boiardi, Dy Booth, Giacomo Boschelle, Elza Burkart, Dan Cadan, Scott Chiddister, Seth Coblentz, Joshua Lee Cooper, Mike Corkery, Sheri Costa, Jérémy Crohet, Malcolm & Parker Curtis, Rose Daily, Robert Dallas, Das Party Paul, Jessica DeMarco-Jacobson, Levi Adam Dollinger, Curtis B. Edmundson, Taneil Eveland, Omar Mansour El-Kikhia, Steven Elsberry, Danielle Evans, Pops Feibel, Dennis Forsgren, Blaine Fucking Fuller, ZM Gentis, GMarkC, Wren Godwin, JC Gonzo, B F Gordon Jr, Dr. Natalie Grand, Frank Hagen, Mahan Harirsaz, Erik Hemming, Aric Herzog, Mark Hoffe, Patrick S Hollingsworth, Jonathan Hope, Shannon Horton, Daniel James, K. Blaine Johnston, Kristiana Josifi, Sis Josip, Haya .K., R. Killmaster, Kurt Johann Klemm, Jeff Lee, Katie & Walter Lee, Giles Leonard, Gardner Linn, Marcus Lopez, J.D. Lowry, Lisalyn M., Marcus, Will Martin, Marci McCann, Jim McElroy, Jack Mearns, Christopher Thomas Medak, Dr. Melvin "Steve" Mesophagus, Dan T. Mjölsness, Noel Montealegre,

Spencer F Montgomery, Gregory Moses, Séamus Murphy, Daniel Pack, Adam Palermo, Alisha Parker-Martell, Andrew Pearson, Bob Plourde, Pedro Ponce, Stephen Press, Cameron Orme, Michael O'Shaughnessy, Poems-For-All, Christopher-Calvin Pollard, Patrick M Regner, D.Roberto, Claire Roddy, Alex Ruiz, Dani Ruiz, Serpent Moon, Joshua De Salis-Sophrin, Kyle Simone, Joon Song, Martin E Stein & Scott A Saxon, Rachel Stephens, Gia Superstar, Paul & Laura Trinies, Dylan Utz, Ben Van Alboom, Cato Vandrare, Ava Vegas, Som Wardner, Jack Waters, Crystal Weber, The Weird Wax Web Dude, Paulie Wenger, Isaiah Whisner, T.R. Wolfe, Vladimir Zaytsev, The Zemenides Family, and Anonymous

www.ingramcontent.com/pod-product-compliance
Lightning Source LLC
Chambersburg PA
CBHW011140290426
44108CB00020B/2697